THE ALPHABET TALE

By Jan Garten | Illustrated by Muriel Batherman

GREENWILLOW BOOKS NEW YORK

Pen and ink and markers
were used for the full-color art.
The text type is Bauer Bodoni.

Text copyright © 1964, renewed
1992, 1994 by Jan Garten.
Illustrations copyright © 1964,
renewed 1992, 1994 by
Muriel Batherman.
First published in 1964
by Random House.
New edition, revised and
re-illustrated, published
in 1994 by Greenwillow Books.

Printed in Singapore
by Tien Wah Press
First Edition
10 9 8 7 6 5 4 3 2 1

Library of Congress
Cataloging-in-Publication Data
Garten, Jan.
The alphabet tale / by Jan Garten;
pictures by Muriel Batherman.
      p.   cm.
ISBN 0-688-12702-9 (trade).
ISBN 0-688-12703-7 (lib. bdg.)
1. Animals—Juvenile literature.
2. English language—Alphabet—
Juvenile literature.
[1. Animals.   2. Alphabet.]
I. Batherman, Muriel, ill.
II. Title.   QL49.G295   1994
591'.022'2—dc20
93-4879   CIP   AC

For David, Daniel, and Alyssa

—J. G.

For Sarah and Allison

—M. B.

Sharp eyes and sharp teeth—
Run first and look later.
This is the tail of an . . .

Alligator

In building dams, she's a great believer.
This is the tail of a busy . . .

Beaver

Softly she walks, pitter pat.
This is the tail of a meowing . . .

Cat

At parties you pin it on him.
Your blindfold won't let you see.
This is the tail of a braying . . .

Donkey

He has two tusks. He has a trunk.

He's big and he's intelligent.

This is the tail of an . . .

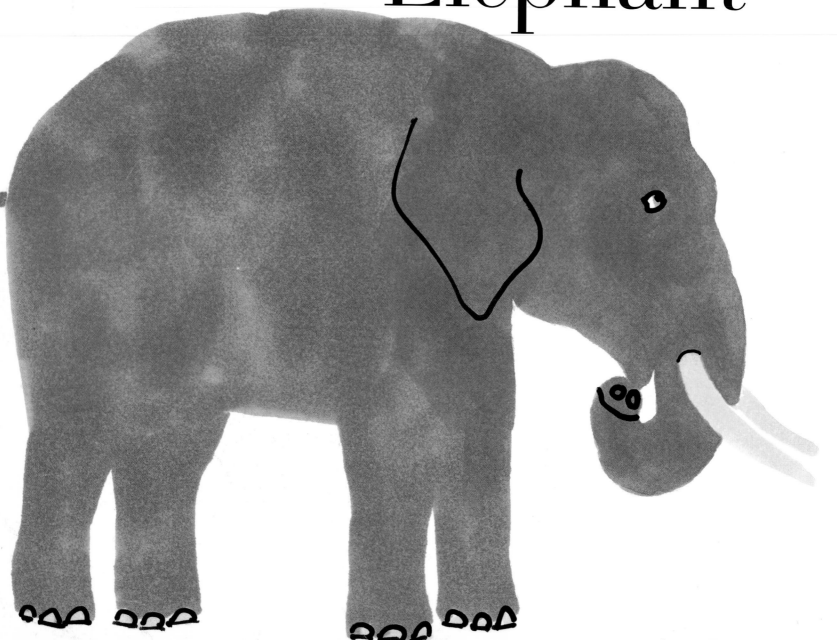

Elephant

A prowler sly chases the flocks.
This is the tail of a wily. . . .

Fox

His neck's so long it makes you laugh.
This is the tail of a tall . . .

Giraffe

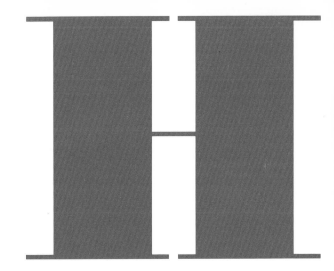

He's a bulky, bathing herbivore.
His appetite is bottomless.
This is the tail of a . . .

Hippopotamus

I

She measures and measures,
squirm by squirm.

This is the tail of a slick . . .

Inchworm

She roams the forest near and far.

This is the tail of a . . .

Jaguar

Watch her hopping round the zoo.
This is the tail of a . . .

Kangaroo

He slinks through the jungle.

He's followed and spied on.

This is the tail of a swift-springing . . .

Lion

M

Swinging high in the branches,
She's playful and spunky.
This is the tail of a mischievous . . .

Monkey

N

She silently slithers along her route.
This is the tail of a slippery . . .

Newt

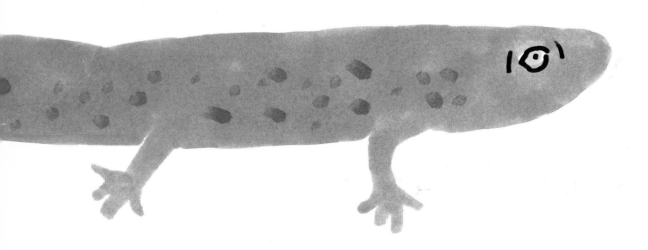

With his head in the sand,

Now which end is which?

This is the tail of a leggy . . .

Ostrich

P

Better beware of each prickly spine.
This is the tail of a . . .

Porcupine

Q

She nests on the ground.
Her feathers are pale.
This is the tail of a cooing . . .

Quail

He looks like the hat of Daniel Boone.

This is the tail of a furry. . . .

Raccoon

His home is the Arctic.
Raw fish is his meal.
This is the tail of a whiskered . . .

Seal

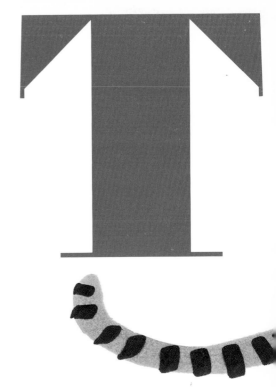

When this feline growls,
Don't walk close by her.
This is the tail of a hungry . . .

Tiger

He's found in make-believe land.
On his forehead is one long horn.
This is the tail of a . . .

Unicorn

V

He swoops on his prey
With his wide wings astir.
This is the tail of a greedy . . .

Vulture

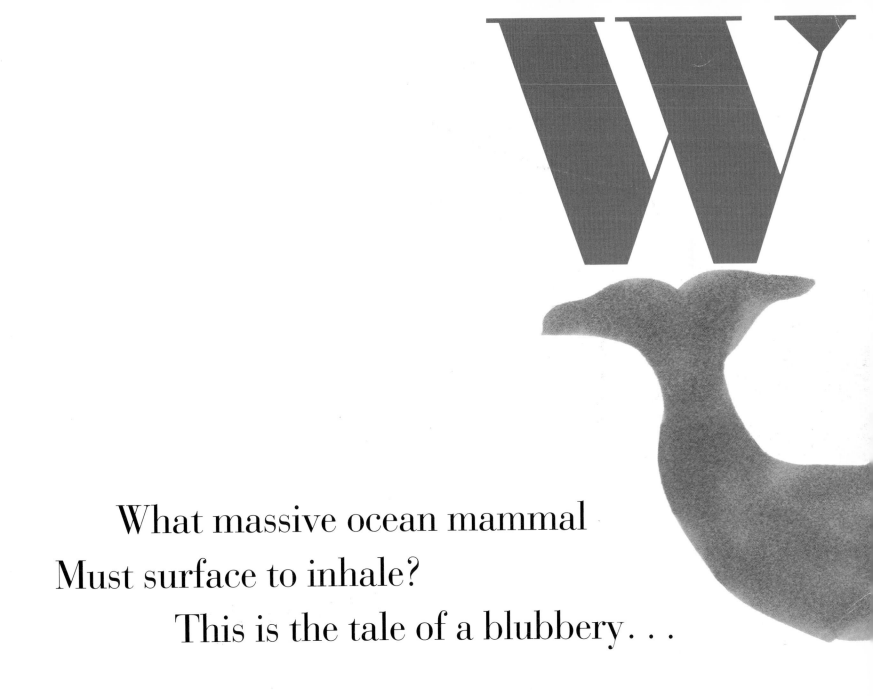

W

What massive ocean mammal
Must surface to inhale?
This is the tale of a blubbery. . .

Whale

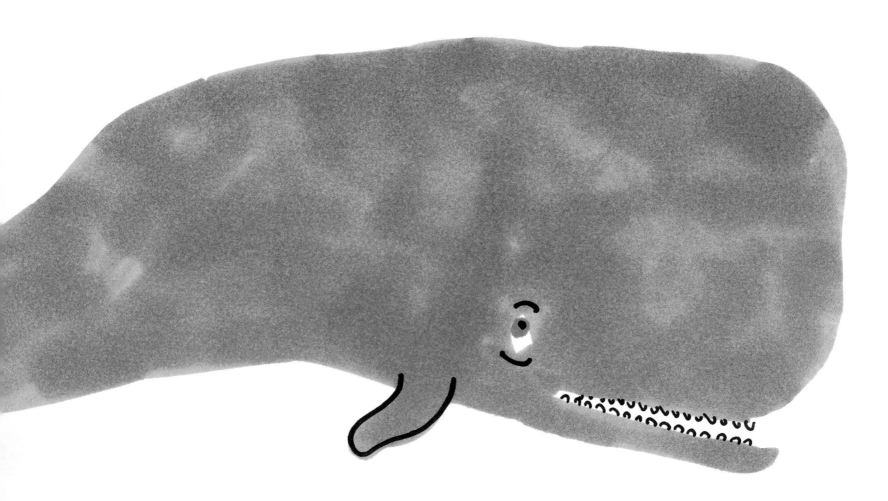

He's an armor-plated animal
 Who lives far away from us.
 This is the tail of a . . .

Xenurus

Yak

She's at home in the cold.

She eats grass for a snack.

This is the tail of a long-haired . . .

Y

She's at home in the cold.

She eats grass for a snack.

This is the tail of a long-haired . . .

Yak

This is the last tail.
Whose tail will it be
    To end the alphabet with a Z?

Zebra